A Beginners' Guide to Forex

The Deep Psychology of Success

Jill Harris

ISBN-13:978-1466439382

ISBN-10:1466439386

Y

"Nobody minds having what is too good for them..."

Jane Austen

About

- Forex is extremely risky – about 90% of those who try to make money online this way – fail!!

- Most traders agree that of those who do succeed – the most important element is psychology. In fact, many people earning a living with forex put their success down to 20% learning and 80% psychology. And because all forms of learning, problem solving and decision making are part of your individual psychology – that means 100% of forex trading success is based on psychology

- Most information about the psychology of trading is vague. Beginners need to know what intellectual tools they can use to enhance their chances of success at forex.

Psychology is the study of human mind and behaviour. It includes areas such as learning, attention, perception, pattern recognition, problem solving and decision making. All key components of being good at anything – including forex.

And it's a disciplined and rigorous academic subject. It requires evidence-based research which tests hypotheses. In other words, a question is asked. Experiments are designed to test that question. The results are analysed to discover the truth.

And it's a new discipline – less than a hundred years old. And the human mind is as complex as the universe. So, we're still on the wagon-trail in a new land when it comes to any real knowledge about what people think – and why they behave the way they do. You know what they used to write on maps when they were clueless about a territory?

'There be dragons.' Which put simply means that anything could live there. Here was a place we didn't understand. Let's imagine it's full of tricksters, monsters and magic. Or manifesting wealth out of nowhere. Or trading foreign currency using your magic wand of patience. Or worse still, believing you can jump into trading straight away if you find the right software...

Scary stuff indeed!

Lack of knowledge also means that the stories early travellers and sailors came out with – were mostly believed. Mermaids, sea-monsters, sirens. You get the picture. What these men were describing were based on real things. Mermaids were probably seals. Sea-monsters – giant squid perhaps. And sirens most likely the haunting song of the great whales – combined with the sexual frustration of a long sea journey.

And let me tell you, most of the stories we tell ourselves about our behaviour are just that.

Stories.

Those who are successful at trading forex – the top 10% - don't really know how to tell you what they're doing. They are correct when they say that it's mostly down to psychology. But because they are natural entrepreneurs (and haven't studied academic psychology in any great detail) – they can't really tell you what or how they're doing it.

Hence a lot of vague advice. Which seems to boil down to this:

- Patience is really important
- Self-discipline is really important too
- Believe you can win (or some other version of magical thinking)

Okay, well yes – patience, self-control and self-belief are necessary – in every area of your life. But they're abstract ideas. They raise more questions than they answer. How do you develop patience? How do you practise self-discipline in foreign currency trading - which is by nature; fast-moving and requires fast decision-making? Why would you believe you can win at forex when so many people fail? And what specific mental processes are involved in creating the right behaviour?

What is the Deep Psychology of Success?

Armed with a burning desire to discover the truth, and a first class degree in psychology – I did what any scientist would do. I searched for the right question. All I had to do was find the answer to that – and then apply it to the subject of currency trading. From the general to the specific – that's how psychologists work.

I found the right question after months of research. It's this: How do you *think* like a successful trader?

And the answer is that successful entrepreneurs in all areas of business are experts at certain types of deep psychological processes. There's been a flurry of recent research in this long-neglected area – and there's still much to be done.

However, there are enough answers to the above question to form a good picture of how to become a success at forex or any other business for that matter.

Once I found this out – I just had to look at the specific area of forex market trading – and apply the findings to that. So, after months of even more research into those who are successful traders – I narrowed their achievements down. They'd stumbled upon an understanding of these five things:

- **It takes time, preparation and planning** – they are never tricked into believing the currency market is a get-rich-quick answer to financial prayers. Cognitive psychology covers this – in other words, problem solving, perception, pattern recognition and decision making...
- **It's exciting and a bit addictive** – great for all you obsessives out there! Passion, excitement, desire – as well as the ability to deal with disappointment - are human emotions – another branch of your psychology that it's crucial to understand before

you start trading

- **It isn't simple** – there is a huge learning curve – a mental challenge that would put Sudoko masers to the test – see cognitive psychology above
- **It's all in the mind!** You'll only succeed if you use certain key psychological processes – *which can be learned* if they don't come naturally to you
- **It's doable.** Otherwise major banks wouldn't rely on it for about 50% of their income!

This book will explore these five areas in detail. Make sure you understand how each of them applies to you as an individual before you put a single penny of your money on the line.

You want to play to win? Of course you do. There's nothing wrong with wanting a little extra money – or even a lot of extra cash. As long as you use it to enhance your own life as well as the lives of those you love!! Personal gain is nothing without good relationships – including a good relationship with yourself. Oh, and once you've got money sorted – you can focus on spiritual development – the path to true happiness (psychologists have studied this in detail too). But I expect you know all that already.

And as Jane Austen points out in Mansfield Park, *"A large income is the best recipe for happiness I ever heard of..."*.

DISCLAIMER:

EVERY EFFORT HAS BEEN MADE TO ACCURATELY PRESENT THE FINDINGS OUTLINED IN THIS BOOK. EVEN THOUGH THIS INDUSTRY IS ONE WHERE SOME PEOPLE CAN WRITE THEIR OWN CHECK IN TERMS OF EARNINGS – THERE IS NO GUARANTEE THAT YOU WILL EARN ANY MONEY USING THE TECHNIQUES AND IDEAS IN THESE MATERIALS. FOREX IS AN EXTREMLY RISKY BUISNESS EXPECIALLY FOR THE LONE TRADER. EXAMPLES IN THESE MATERIALS ARE NOT TO BE INTERPRETED AS A PROMISE OR GUARANTEE OF EARNINGS. EARNINGS POTENTIAL IS ENTIRELY DEPENDENT ON THE PERSON USING THIS BOOK AND THE IDEAS AND TECHNIQUES CONTAINED THEREIN. WE DO NOT PROPOSE THAT THIS IS A GET-RICH-QUICK SCHEME.

ANY CLAIMS MADE OF ACTUAL EARNINGS OR EXAMPLES OF ACTUAL RESULTS CAN BE VERIFIED UPON REQUEST. YOUR LEVEL OF SUCCESS IN ATTAINING RESULTS CLAIMED IN OUR MATERIALS DEPENDS ON THE TIME YOU DEVOTE TO THE PROGRAM, IDEAS AND TECHNIQUES MENTIONED, YOUR FINANCES, KNOWLEDGE AND SKILLS. SINCE THESE FACTORS DIFFER ACCORDING TO INDIVIDUALS WE CANNOT GUARANTEE YOUR SUCCESS OR INCOME LEVEL. NOR ARE WE RESPONSIBLE FOR ANY OF YOUR ACTIONS.

MATERIALS IN OUR PRODUCT AND OUR WEBSITE MAY CONTAIN INFORMATION THAT INCLUDES OR IS BASED UPON FORWARD-LOOKING STATEMENTS. FORWARE-LOOKING STATEMENTS GIVE OUR EXPECTATIONS OR FORECASTS OF

FUTURE EVENTS. YOU CAN IDENTIFY THESE STATEMENTS BY THE FACT THAT THEY DO NOT RELATE STRICTLY TO HISTORICAL OR CURRENT FACTS. THEY USE WORDS SUCH AS 'ANTICIPATE'; 'ESTIMATE', 'EXPECT', 'PROJECT', 'INTEND', 'PLAN', 'BELIEVE', AND OTHER WORDS AND TERMS OF SIMILAR MEANING IN CONNECTION WITH A DESCRIPTION OF POTENTIAL EARNINGS OR FINANCIAL PERFORMANCE.

ANY AND ALL FORWARD-LOOKING STATEMENTS HERE OR ON ANY OF OUR SALES MATERIAL ARE INTENDED TO EXPRESS OUR OPINION OF EARNINGS POTENTIAL. MANY FACTORS WILL BE IMPORTANT IN DETERMINING YOUR ACTUAL RESULTS AND NO GUARANTEES ARE MADE THAT YOU WILL ACHIEVE RESULTS. IN FACT, NO GUARANTEES ARE MADE THAT YOU WILL ACHIEVE ANY RESULTS FROM OUR IDEAS AND TECHNIQUES.

Contents:

Introduction: What is forex trading – and does it really work?

Chapter One: Why is a knowledge of deep psychology essential when trading forex?

Chapter Two: The 3 roots of greed - failing with forex – and how to avoid it.

Chapter Three: The 4 steps to forex success.

Chapter Four: The Deep Psychology of Trading Part 1: learn how to think like a successful trader.

Chapter Five: The Deep Psychology of Trading Part 2: how to trade in the long term – the social psychology of forex trading.

Conclusion.

Introduction:

What is forex trading – and does it really work?

What is forex?

Forex trading is the buying and selling of **currencies** on the international market. It's the largest market in the world and currently about $2 trillion changes hands every day!!! Hmm, that's a lot of money sloshing around waiting to be mopped up by those in the know.

Up until about ten years ago the only real players in forex were the banks, governments and some rather shadowy hedge funds.

It's an extremely volatile market. The changes in exchange rates can be quite dramatic on any given day. Changes are measured in **pips** – usually the fourth number after the decimal point. You trade in pairs, buying one currency and selling another at the same time.

The pips tell you what the difference is between your two currencies. So, if one currency is worth 5.0001 against the value of its partner at the start of a trade – and you're lucky enough to sell it for 5.0031 at the end – you've made a killing! On the other hand, if you've done it the other way round – oh dear.

To make this clearer, let's say you're going on a skiing holiday in Switzerland. You've got 10 American dollars in your hand and you want to sell them – and buy Swiss francs. Last week you might have got 7.95 Swiss francs in the deal. Today you got 7.94. The Swiss franc has fallen because there's been a riot in Geneva (highly unlikely I know, but this is just an example). When you only need a few francs it doesn't matter a whole hill of beans.

But what if you sold $100 and got CHF 79.95 – when last week you could've got CHF 80.77? Well, you've lost a small amount but so what? And what if it's worked the other way round – and you've got more francs for your dollar this week? That kind of a difference won't even buy you a cup of coffee. Not in that part of the world at any rate.

Okay, imagine this instead:

What if every one dollar you invested – you actually traded as if it was one hundred dollars?

That's what happens when you trade in forex. The initial investment is given what is called **'leverage'**. Too much leverage can be dangerous. It's often what gets people into trouble.

Who gives you leverage?

Leverage is what you get from a broker. An individual trader like you has to go through a forex **broker.** The broker offers you leverage – like our example of 100-1. So, when you trade it's as if your money is multiplied by a hundred or two hundred and so on.

This is where it begins to look like gambling. And to a certain extent, playing any market – like investing in stocks and shares is a gamble. A broker who wants to fleece you of all your worldly goods might offer you 500-1 as leverage. Warning: *There be dragons.* Especially if you're new to forex. If you win – great. And that's what might tempt you to accept this kind of deal. But if you lose... there will be tears and worse. You might lose everything.

However, if you learn the techniques of deep psychology – you'll develop a plan that protects you against gambling-style thinking.

Does forex really work?

In other words - Is it worth getting involved in such a volatile and risky market?

Well, yes and no. There's a great deal of disagreement on this issue. Some people say it's no place for a lone trader sitting on her computer at home watching the signals and eating a doughnut.

Signals, by the way, are the signs you've got to read and understand in order to make a decision about when to buy and when to sell.

Basically signals indicate what your chosen currency pair is doing and what it did in the past. Don't worry too much about that now, we'll cover the basic forex terminology later. So, the main argument against getting involved in forex is that it's just too fast-moving and complex for an individual trader.

But. there are also a lot of people (the top 10% of people who do make money at forex) who think it's a great market to be in. They do actually make a decent amount of extra cash doing this. But don't forget - most of those who are making money with forex are the old hands – banks, hedge fund managers etc. These people were often in the game way before it opened its doors to any Tina, Daisy and Harriet who fancied a go.

However, it's worth noting that even if the successful ordinary folk trading forex are only a tiny minority of a tiny minority– *they are making it work.* And it's pretty new territory for most of us – so we're still trying to figure it out. The successful ones have got one thing in common though – and they all talk about it – even if they can't explain it.

What do they say is the main foundation of their success?

Yup, you've guessed it. They call it psychology. Social scientists would say they've got their deep psychology in order. What if you knew how to do this? What if you knew what mental processes were involved and knew how to act at every stage of your forex journey? And what if you could trade like them?   Well, then it most certainly would be worth getting involved.

To recap: Forex is the biggest market in the world. Ordinary people can now get involved.

Remember that it's a market which operates in pairs. You buy and sell two different currencies simultaneously – just like you do when you go abroad on vacation.

Leverage makes your money grow – but only if you do a good trade. Brokers do the deal and offer you leverage. All your decisions are based on how you read the signals.

In the end *only you can decide* if forex is a market you truly want to be in.

Don't worry though. You can make this decision with ease by reading on. When you get to the chapter on thinking like a successful trader, you'll be able to assess if its really the right business for you to be in.

Chapter One:

Why is a knowledge of deep psychology essential when trading forex?

There are three general areas of psychology it's essential to understand in order to plan a successful foray into forex:

- Information processing – including pattern recognition, problem solving, attention, perception and decision-making
- Personality – including character traits, types, strengths and weaknesses
- Memory – learning

Cognitive psychology is the way you process information

We process information from the outside world constantly. In fact, the objects and everything else we see around us are not solid shapes at all. They consist of a bunch of whirling atoms bouncing around at various speeds. When you look at a table you see a consistent shape. This is because your brain has done some wonderful calculations and come up with 'table'.

Let's say you walk into a room you've never been in before. In your hand is a hot cup of coffee. You're tired and you just want to sit down and have your drink in peace. What does your brain do?

Brain focuses your **attention** on the area of the room containing a 'table-like' object

Copyright Jill Harris © 2011

Brain **perceives** that this object is similar to other objects you've come across in the past which are the same basic 'table-like' shape

- Brain double-checks and recognises the **pattern** a thing called 'table' makes against its background – and you can see that this object is stable
- You've **solved the problem** of where to put your cup of coffee – because this is not only a table - but it's also not wobbly and therefore your drink won't slide off it
- You **make a decision** to sit down at the table and drink your coffee
- You go through the same process to work out a chair-like object!

You may be wondering what the heck this has to do with forex trading. Simple. You make or break based on how you analyse charts, economic climates, technical information and signals. These are the signs you have to read, process, understand and act on. You make a trade based on your level of understanding of these signs – and your memory of everything you've learned about <u>what those signs and signals mean to you</u>.

So, here are those processes again – but this time they take place when you're thinking of making a forex trade:

- Brain focuses your **attention** on the area of the screen where you spot a 'good-trading-situation' object
- Brain **perceives** that this object is similar to other objects you've come across in the past which are the same basic 'good-trading-situation' shape
- Brain double-checks, recognises the **pattern** a thing called 'good-trading-situation'

makes against its background – and you can see that this object might earn you some money

- You've **solved the problem** of when to do the trade – because this is not only a good-trading-situation - but you have the means to support a loss if this occurs...
- You make a decision to buy or sell – whichever is appropriate.

And you do all of this in a matter of seconds. Wow! The brain really is a marvellous thing. And cognition isn't even the half of it. But for now let's look more closely at how this happens in the mind of an accomplished trader.

When she pays attention to the emerging patterns in the forex charts, reads the signals and sets her stop-loss margins, she knows exactly what she's looking for. This is because she's using deep psychological processing to make her decisions – and practised this skill over and over again.

Learning is the easy part. You only have to learn the basics once. Commit the buzzwords, meanings and facts about forex to memory. Of course, a wise trader is always open to learning more – building on past knowledge and creating an inner database of forex expertise.

But what about practise? The beginner at forex should **always** spend time practising on a demo platform. Most brokers will provide you with an account – full of fake money – with which you can practise, practise, practise...

You wouldn't go and play guitar in front of a live audience if you hadn't practised would you? Same with forex. Never be tempted to put your money down immediately by promises of a system which does the thinking for you. You have to be able to do the thinking first – even if you do use an automated system later on to help you make decisions.

I hope you can see by now why it's really helpful to understand the way you think – before you even begin looking around at forex markets. And it should also be clear by now that you're going to need to study – hard. You'll need to get the knowledge first so you know which patterns to look out for and what the various signals mean.

And then you need to test your knowledge with a demo platform with fake money.

Remember – you weren't born knowing what a table is. You had to learn what sorts of shapes to pay attention to, how to perceive table-like object, recognise the patterns of a stable table – and rely on memory to work out what you could do with it.

Now you do it automatically. But what about your personality?

Why is personality important when it comes to trading in forex?

Your character is the make or break factor when it comes to success in forex. It's the kind of deep psychology you have to understand fully. Interestingly, no single personality type is more successful than any other.

So, it doesn't mater what type of person you are. What matters is how you work with your own characteristics.

For example, if you're a naturally enthusiastic person you'll need to watch out that you don't jump in too quickly with your own money.

A friendly person might be much more successful if he does forex with a friend. They can bounce ideas off each other.

A creative type will be able to use her creativity to plan a killer strategy for analysing signs and signals. And so on.

The next chapter looks at how you can find out what kind of person you are. There's also an explanation of how each character can play to their strengths in forex – and avoid their weak points getting in the way of a successful trade.

Memory and learning – techniques and tips

As you've probably worked out by now, you'll need to devote a serious amount of brain power to learning about forex at the beginning. Memory is a huge subject in psychology. I won't go on about the theories or the brain chemistry involved. All you need to know is how to work with your own memory so you learn fast and well.

Oh, and if you don't like learning stuff you better get out of forex right now!! It isn't hard – but it is a challenge. So, prepare yourself for a period of serious study.

How to study properly

Learning is different for everybody. My son learns just by reading the information he needs to know. He's lucky. Most of us have to work with the information until we've got it in long-term memory and can use it.

Here's what you need to do:

- Find a good course and work through it
- Keep a notebook of your progress – writing your notes by hand helps learning
- Ask questions – don't move on until you understand the answer

You don't have to pay for a course...

You can learn all you need to know for free on the internet.

There's a brilliant step by step course in forex on this website: www.babypips.com – and I highly recommend working through their material.

The reason it's so good is because they've broken up the subject into chunks. Your memory likes chunks. It can't digest a mountain of information in one go. It sort of shuts down and doesn't take it in. But when there are small manageable chunks – memory can sort it all out bit by bit.

Your memory works by creating tiny pathways – neural pathways of electrical patterns through to the required information storage area. Think of these like paths in the woods. At first, they're hardly visible. If you walk the same route a lot, the path becomes clearer. Deeper. You learn the way. If you walk the path once with a quick read-through, you'll be heading for disaster.

Take your time. Better still – take notes. Hand-written notes are best. Go out and buy a notebook. Your brain has to take in the information in a physical and personal way if you write by hand. It gives you time to absorb.

Ask questions.

Don't move on until you've got the answer.

What don't you understand? Are pips a mystery to you? Write out a specific question about pips in your notebook. What exactly is mysterious about pips to you? By doing this, you're exploring the subject in your own way.

Questioning is the art, heart and soul of learning. Look up the answer. Or go on one of the forums, *babypips* has a good one, and ask the question in the newbie area.

Tricks and tips to help you learn

Music – play whatever music lights your fire while you study. Then, when you're trading forex, play the music in the background. Plenty of studies have shown this works a treat.

Copyright Jill Harris © 2011

Oh, and it doesn't have to be Mozart. If thrash metal is your thing – go with that.

Sticky Notes – write out the main buzzwords and a brief explanation on stickies and pop them on the inside of cupboard doors or all over one wall if you like. The brain can't help reading. Even if you're not concentrating on the words, your brain is reading them anyway.

Perfume/Aftershave – yes, this works really well. Wear a particular scent while you study. Then, when you come to trading – make sure you've sprayed some on. The sense of smell is the first one activated in the womb – and the last to go when we die. It has links to memory we don't yet understand properly – but use it to your advantage.

Exercise – while you're walking, running, dancing or working-out – go over the main points you've been studying. If you use your body as part of the learning experience it goes deep – especially if you work out regularly.

Discuss – for most of us – it helps to talk over a new subject with another person. Not just on the newbie forums, but also face to face with a patient friend or partner. Better yet, start a little forex group – if you're a group kind of a person, it'll be an enormous source of support - both intellectually and emotionally.

Meditation – I will keep banging on about this!! It really does help to clear your mind of clutter before you start a session of study. If you're studying online go and have a look at some of the lovely meditation videos on youtube.

Attitude – remember often why you're doing this. It's a means to an end so you might as well enjoy it. The world of forex is not just about signals and analysis. Successful traders never lose sight of why they're doing what they're doing. This is the key to motivation.

Economic Awareness – forex is totally connected to what's going on in the economies of different countries. It's about social, cultural and political tides. Figure out how certain changes – for example an election – can effect the currency. Know that by watching the news with forex awareness you're also continuing your studies. And by trading in forex you're somehow taking part in the great global roller-coaster ride of history in the making.

And one last note of caution. If studying forex isn't any fun for you – stop doing it at the learning phase.

Chapter Two:

The 3 roots of greed – why most people fail at forex – and how you can avoid it

'What wild imaginations one forms where dear self is concerned! How sure to be

mistaken!'

Jane Austen

Greed and out-of-control risk-taking are the two main pitfalls of forex traders. They act on them because they misunderstand the deep psychology of success.

As we said earlier, leverage is often the downfall of newbie fx traders. It amounts to a temptation to lose control and trade in a random. Remember the woolly advice about self-discipline? Translate that as 'don't be greedy' or 'don't lose control'.

However, it's all too easy to slip into a mind-set of greed or chaotic risk-taking without realising what's happening. Until it's too late. As I said, it's a volatile market – and highly addictive. If you've been trading at a loss – you'll naturally want to put it right. Your adrenaline high increases – an inexperienced trader may well react to the market instead of being controlled and calm. That's how they crash and burn.

A lot of forex gurus advise you to 'avoid taking big risks' as though it's the same as being greedy. It isn't. Greed and risk-taking are two very different kinds of psychological process.

The emotional pull of greed

When you think about it - the offer of high leverage opens up a world of possibilities for the individual trader. You could end up with a huge amount of money. Piles of the stuff. This idea grows in your mind. You start to imagine what you will do with all that dosh, wonga, dollar in the hand. You take on too much leverage. Before you know it, you're on the road to financial loss.

The thing is - greed has its roots in three very different areas of your deep psychology even though they lead to similar behaviours. The behaviour manifests as risk-taking when trading. But the three roots of greed are:

- A desperate need to pay bills or service debt - ***anxiety***
- An innate love of taking risks – adrenaline junkie ***personality type***
- A desire to impress others – often indicating a weak ***ego***

Lets' have a look at the deep psychology of the two forces outlined above.

Anxiety

Anxiety-driven behaviour due to external conditions – such as the very stressful situation of debt – is incredibly bad for your decision-making ability. Money fuels our lives.

Debt creates a threatening situation which is translated by your primitive brain as 'danger'. You go on red alert.

Adrenaline pumps. Blood is moved away from areas you don't really need to use such as the brain. This is because anxiety or fear causes the fight or flight reflex. You don't need a lot of oxygen in your brain to fight. Or to run. You need it in your muscles.

In the twenty-first century money worries can't be sorted out by fighting or sprinting away at the speed of light. You might think your nervous energy is giving you clarity. It's a myth. If you're trading with money you can't really afford to lose – you thinking with fear instead of realism. More adrenaline is released.

Therefore, you're likely to make mistakes.

How to avoid anxiety-driven greed

Number one is to take a good, hard look at your life. If you've got money problems now, playing the forex market won't help. Deal with the problems right in front of you first by:

- Sorting out immediate issues such as unpaid bills
- Seek help if you're already in debt – from a trustworthy source
- Don't borrow money to play the forex

- Discover your personality type – and if you're prone to anxiety – find ways to work on that before you start trading with real money!
- Above all, make peace with yourself!

Making peace with yourself is about observing your thoughts... and letting them go.

A wise man once told me to get the spiritual stuff sorted out first – then everything else would follow. He was *not* talking about religion. He was talking about an approach to life in general. A sort of an 'inside out' way of living.

Most people's behaviour is the result of unconscious mechanisms. No, we're not getting into Freud too much here, but he was right about the power of the unconscious mind to motivate us to act out in certain ways.

Anxiety is fear. Fear is a useful emotion in certain situations. It's a warning that something is wrong. However, fear-based anxiety can often work against you. Especially in a situation where you're going to need clarity of mind. And that's what you need to trade foreign exchange successfully.

How to gain clarity of mind

Number one: learn how to meditate – if you don't know already. No need to go in for long sessions of chanting and religious rituals if you don't want to. Just learn how to sit and breathe and most important of all:

Observe your thoughts.

There are plenty of great websites featuring simple breathing meditation techniques – but here's the most basic and powerful one I know:

- Get comfortable – sit cross-legged if you like, or lie down
- Relax the muscles in your body by noticing where there is tension and letting it go
- Take three deep breaths
- Focus on the rise and fall of your breathing
- Notice any thoughts that come along
- Don't try and control them or think about nothing
- Observe the thoughts – but don't get hung up on them
- Imagine all your thoughts, moods, emotions and desires are transient – they come and go, rise and fall just like your breathing
- Once you've watched a thought move on, focus on your breath again

Do this once a day for about five minutes. Build up to ten or twenty minutes if you can. There is a whole heap of good, solid psychological research that shows meditation of this kind is one of the best methods for dealing with anxiety and developing clarity of mind.

Clarity of mind is essential to your success.

If you notice that anxiety is affecting your performance at any stage in your forex dealings, stop, go sit on your mat and meditate.

To avoid getting into a cycle of anxiety-greed-mistakes - make sure you follow the planning guide to forex success in the next chapter. There, you'll be shown how to create a plan which includes a money-management system you can cope with.

Oh, and be sure you don't ever take on more leverage than you can afford to lose!!!

Personality Type

Part of the deep psychology of success in forex is to know and understand how to work with your personality type. There are several main theories about how to measure personality type out there. We don't need to go into a lengthy discussion about the pros and cons of each one.

If you want to think like a successful forex trader you've got to know your 'self'. Who are you and in what ways do you interact with the world?

Exercise: Grab a piece of paper and write down 'who am I?' at the top. Now list twenty things.

Most of us will list more roles, groups and achievements than personality traits. You might describe yourself as a daughter, father, son, auntie, middle-aged or teen. You may have

Copyright Jill Harris © 2011

listed your membership of a club, job title or qualifications.

All these things are good – and they do say something about you. However, the reason most people don't write down their personality traits is because they don't really know who they are!!

How to avoid personality-fuelled mistakes

Play to your strengths.

Work with forex and not against it by using your natural skills and talents. Personality traits can be your greatest deep psychological weapon when it comes to trading fx. Know where you are strong and use your power to plan, prepare and practise forex trading.

To be a success at forex or any other business – you must know who you are – otherwise how will you play to your strengths?

Over the past twenty years, I've researched all the available personality theories and tried out just about all the relevant tests and there is one that is head and shoulders above the rest. It's called the Enneagram. You can take a free personality test by visiting the main site of the enneagram institute here:

http://www.enneagraminstitute.com

Of course we're all a mixture of types – but one personality type will be dominant. Find out what your dominant type is and make a note of how you operate in the world. If you play to the strengths of your type – you'll be far more likely to succeed.

Here's a list of the nine enneagram types and how each one might work best in terms of forex trading:

1. **The Reformer:** Because you're rational and an idealist – you'll work best by keeping detailed notes on each stage of your progress with forex. You'll enjoy keeping spreadsheets up to date, managing your money carefully and most important of all – learning everything you need to know before you are ready to invest any money. On a bad day you might become impatient – so watch out for that. Meditation is your friend! Also, as a perfectionist – be aware that you might have issues with accepting loss. Everyone makes mistakes. Pin this one your wall: "It's not how much you lose when you make an error of judgement – it's how much you gain when you get it right."

2. **The Helper:** Above all, you're a people person. Because you're great with others – you'll work best by forming a forex group. You might start off with one friend or a partner – and perhaps build it from there. By learning together and discussing the movements in currencies, you'll feel more comfortable than if you try and go it alone. On a bad day you might be tempted to suffer alone rather than bother anyone with your problems. Don't! Share the lows as well as the highs, for a healthy, successful forex approach.

3. **The Achiever:** Because you've got a clear sense of self-belief and you're highly

Copyright Jill Harris © 2011

motivated you'll be able to put these characteristics to good use trading fx. Your drive will keep you going through the long learning phase, and you'll keep a steady eye on your trading goals. On a bad day you might get obsessive – staying up late and pushing too hard to win back your losses. Don't! Be aware of your emotional responses – and flag up when you're on the edge of losing control. Set your exits and don't widen the gap. And get some sleep.

4. **The Individualist:** Because you've highly self-aware you'll find it easy to tap into your feelings and avoid getting over-anxious or fear-driven during a trade. Your sensitivity will be put to good use in judging the subtle changes in the markets. Also, you'll be able to make good use of the economic news from the countries whose currencies you're trading in. An artistic temperament is well-suited to forex trading – whatever anyone might say! On a bad day you'll be prone to indulging in self-pity. Stop! If you're feeling devasted after a bad trade, get some sleep, fresh air or do something creative which isn't forex.

5. **The Investigator:** Because you're able to concentrate for long periods of time, forex will be a good environment for you to use these natural skills to the max. Your curiosity will enable you to seek answers to all your questions before you move into trading with real money. And if you utilise your ability to see the world in different way from most others – you'll be able to step back and understand global markets very well indeed. This personality type will probably take the longest time to choose a broker and open a demo account. This tendency to study any new subject in detail is a huge benefit when it comes to forex. On a bad day you might be tempted to isolate yourself and try to work things out alone. Stop! You need to talk to someone about what's happening. Make sure at least one other person knows

about your forex experiences.

6. **The Loyalist:** Because you're ultimately security-oriented you are the least likely personality type to jump into forex live trading with high leverage for quick gains. Take advantage of your natural stability and courage to forge a steady path towards your goals. Also, use your excellent troubleshooting skills to solve problems before they become overwhelming. On a bad day you'll be prone to anxiety-driven trading. Be aware of this. Stop! Don't just keep on reacting to a negative situation. Meditate and relax.

7. **The Enthusiast:** Because of your naturally high levels of optimism you'll find goal-setting easy and self-belief in bucket-loads. Your natural playfulness can be put to good use during the forex demo account stage when you'll be trading with fake money. By resisting distractions you'll be able to set achievable goals – and are most likely to really enjoy your trading experiences. On a bad day you're likely to become scattered and impulsive – capable of making careless mistakes due to impatience. Stop! Meditation will quiet your mind and overcome impatient impulses.

8. **The Challenger:** Because you're naturally self-confident and assertive, you'll be able to make sure you get the time and resources you need to go the distance with forex. Scams won't last long with you. And if you do fall prey to an unscrupulous broker or overpriced automatic system - you'll deal with it – no problem. On a bad day – you're likely to get angry rather than fearful. Stop! Don't take a few losses out on those around you. Go for a run or a long walk.

9. **The Peacemaker:** With your easy-going attitude, stability and creativity – you've got a deep well of excellent character traits you can use in the planning, preparation and practise stages of your forex journey. Your friendly personality makes it a good

move for you too to trade forex with a friend or in a group so you can share tips and hints about forex with others. On a bad day you're likely to freeze up and downplay your losses. Stop! Don't give up. Be realistic about what is going on. Go back to demo trading with fake money and analyse your mistakes before you use real money again.

How to avoid weak ego driven greed...

Okay, let's get one thing clear. Ego is a neutral term. It's YOU.

<u>Your ego is simply the self you present to the world</u>. It's made up of your personality, upbringing and experiences.   The term 'ego' is often used misguidedly used to put someone down. People might say 'he's got a big ego...' when what they actually mean is 'he's really arrogant.'

Your ego is either healthy or weak. A healthy ego will protect you from self-delusion. In forex you can delude yourself into thinking that if you stay up all night you'll make the trade you want.

Or a weak ego might believe that if you take on enormous leverage – you'll be able to buy a flash car and impress your friends. A person with a weak ego will have the kind of friends that will be impressed by material possessions.   Status is everything to an unhealthy ego – since it has no depth to draw on.

A healthy ego will want to achieve balance in all areas of her life. She'll know that money can buy her more time with the people she loves. She'll be realistic enough to know that a true money-making venture has to be approached as a business. A business takes time, effort and learning to get off the ground. There will losses along the way and she'll factor them in.

How to create a healthy ego..

You've already taken the first step by examining your personality type. Use this self-knowledge to get to grips with your weak areas. As well as using your strengths to plan, prepare and practise.

The deep psychology of a healthy ego is this – admit your weaknesses – and take responsibility for them. A person with a weak ego will blame everyone else for his mistakes. He won't get far trading forex because he'll think he's doing fine. When he makes a loss it'll be the fault of the software or the broker or the baby crying. Nothing is ever his fault.

Be honest with yourself. A strong ego accepts that no one is perfect. A weak ego can't bear to be vulnerable or guilty of making bad decisions. This is why so many people with weak egos appear to have high self-esteem. They create an illusion of superiority to others in order to boost the essential emptiness of their inner lives.

Deepen the experience of your inner life by taking time to read, love and walk in nature.

Watch films with substance. You don't have to do this all the time, just make sure you're as comfortable with your own company as you are when you're with others. Often a person with a weaker ego struggles to spend time alone.

A healthy ego will have a good, honest opinion of her own abilities. This is **essential** to a successful approach to forex trading. I can't stress that enough. Being honest with yourself means you'll know if you've done the work of planning and are ready to go on to using a demo forex system. Your assessment of your self-competency will be close to the mark. And your analysis of the feasibility of trading forex – when it comes to a balance of risk and your own competency – won't fail you.

A strong ego will also be honest enough to assess her progress with an open mind. If she's not ready to go on to the next phase – she'll spend more time learning. If she's losing money – she'll go back to learning.

A person with a weaker ego needs to work closely with his or her deep psychology in order to gain success. A good way of doing this is to learn as much as you can about your personality type. The official Enneagram website is a great way to start. Better still, get a hold of the book written by the developers of this theory.

In it you'll find charts and guidelines about how to avoid falling into unhealthy patterns – and which ones are the biggest problems for your character. Oh, and you can start another notebook – this one focussing on your self-development.

It's a lovely thought that in the pursuit of an extra income – you have to grow as a person too!

Chapter Three: How to be a successful trader

4 steps to success

Okay, well - so far we've looked at the cognitive processes of forex trading, the 3 main psychological pitfalls of the beginner forex trader, and finding your personality type.

So let's focus on the 4 steps to success.

Each step builds on the last one, and it's important to do them in order. Having said that, one of the most crucial and challenging steps is learning. Forex trading, like any other business involves *learning all the time*. Keep up with the current news, views, charts and signals. Join a good online forum or local forex group and become an active member.

You never stop learning - because you're dealing with an ever-changing environment. The psychology of learning is a big subject. I've given you the basic tools, tips and techniques. But you should find out what works best for you – especially if you've been out of education for a while.

Perhaps you're a practical person – if so – keep your learning focused on 'doing' something. If you're a bit of a geek, read everything you can about forex from good sources.

In a fluid, fast-moving environment like forex trading – it really helps if you work on having a flexible, open-minded approach to every trade you make. You need to learn from each mistake as well as your successes.

Remember: your mistakes will teach you more.

Here are the 4 steps to succes with forex. If you follow them closely, there is no reason why you can't become one of the top 10% who do actually make extra cash– if not a living - from this market.

- Step One: Planning: Goals, outlines and realistic expectations...
- Step Two: Playfulness: A beginners guide to signals...
- Step Three: Preparing to trade with real money...
- Step Four: Practical assessment: How are you doing – honestly?

Step One: Planning: Goals, outlines and realistic expectations...

Get out your forex notebook and get comfortable. This is a time for reflection. On a clean page write out your overall trading plan.

Use the following suggestions as a springboard for your outline.

First plan out how you as an individual will work your trading strategy. To begin with, write out a character assessment outline something like this:

My character Type

I'm a (-----------)

therefore I'll use my strength in (---------) to work the market.

I should avoid my weakness towards (-----------------) by being aware of it and knowing when I should stop!

Goals

Next, copy down this list of goals word for word. Writing is a powerful thing. It sets something in motion. WARNING: if you don't do this step you are in danger of making serious mistakes and losing money. Go ahead, write the words on the page and make a decision to act on them.

My Goals

I will be realistic about how much money I expect to make.

I will be realistic about how much money I can afford to lose.

41   *Copyright Jill Harris © 2011*

I will spend at least one month learning the basics.

I will open a demo account and practise trading the forex until I'm successful at it for at least three months in a row...

I will research brokers until I find a reliable one.

I will start trading with a small amount of money – and with a low (50-1 or 100-1) leverage until I've successfully made a profit for three months in a row.

If I make a loss, I'll stop. I won't throw any more of my hard-earned cash at it until I've gone back to the demo platform and worked through my mistakes.

I'll earn enough money to start trading again – I won't go into debt in order to play the market.

If I start making crazy trades and staying up late until I'm exhausted, I'll stop and go back to the beginning. I'll work out who I am, what character traits are affecting my trading and get some sleep.

I'm in it to make a profit...

I will keep notes of my forex progress, the highs and lows – and above all – I'll manage my money well...

Next – create an outline strategy for a realistic, feasible approach to forex

It should include these points:

- First – decide how much money you can invest in forex
- Second – outline your level of risk – in other words – how much are you able to lose when trading – without getting into trouble.
- Third – whatever number you wrote down for steps one and two, halve it!
- Fourth – choose one currency pair to focus on Here are the best ones to start with if you're a beginner:
    - EUR/USD (Euro/US dollar)
    - GBP/USD (British pound/US dollar)
    - USD/JPY (US dollar/Japanese yen)
- It probably helps to choose a currency from a country you live in or whose economics interest you as one of the pair.
- Fourth – make sure are able to devote at least two hours a week to studying the basics of forex – and at least the same again in finding out what is happening in the economies of the currencies of your chosen pair.

Step Two: Playfulness: A beginners guide to signals...

Here's a quick run-down of what forex signals are and how to use them. Signals are basically a call to action. They're a recommendation to make a trade – according to the currency pair you're working with.

Signals are based on different types of analysis of the market and they take place in real time. If you decide to work with a signals service - you'll be alerted via SMS, tweets or some other fast delivery service.

Some signals providers use complex mathematical formulae – algorithms – to calculate their suggestions. These can be based on several types of analysis, namely:

Technical – a look at the historical movements of the market based on price changes in the past. Most signals use this technique. It's useful up to a point – although it's worth remembering that any global market is basically unpredictable.

Fundamental – this kind of analysis is more in-depth. It looks at past and present actions on the market and includes things like the current economic and social situations in the country or countries using a particular currency. As you can see already – this is probably a more useful form of analysis and so signals from this source might be more reliable.

Sentimental – this type of analysis looks at what people are thinking about the market! It's based on surveys – so it's called 'sentimental' because it's about how people feel. If the general feeling is that the market is going up – the trader goes against in the opposite direction. So, buy when others are selling and sell when others are feeling like buying.

Copyright Jill Harris © 2011

More on this later when we look at the social psychology of global trading.

You might be wondering right now what all this stuff has to do with playfulness. Well, a lot really.

Playing around with signals on a demo platform with fake money is a great way to develop your own forex style. You are not a robot – unlike many of the automate expert advisors out there. Before you decide what kind of signals you're going to use, find out what works for you.

Learning goes much deeper if you're fascinated by something. If you love numbers – play around with your own versions of technical analysis. If numbers are not your thing at all, discover the joys of fundamental analysis – and look out for sentimental surveys.

Once you've messed around with signals for a while you'll find you understand what they are and how they work.

Now it's time to choose a signals service provider.

DANGER: Many scams out there will try to sell you overpriced, overcomplicated signals services.

How to choose a signals service that works for you:

The simplest and most sensible way for the beginner is use free signals while you're playing on the demo site.

Best advice is to go a great website like www.forexpeacearmy.com and have a look at their free signals service. It's easy to use and worth a try. More than that, this site has a load of reviews about paid signals services – including robots, expert advisors etc. These reviews are reliable and will give you the real deal on who is out to rip you off and who will offer you a good service.

If you start forex right and learn all about the market, make your outline plan and stay with the demo until you've done three solid months of profitable trading – you'll have got the hang of signals and your confidence will be high.

Later on, you'll probably be confident enough to set out your own signals parameters using your knowledge and experience of different kinds of analysis.

Make sure you've been realistic about how much money you've got to invest and go on to the next stage.

Step Three: Preparing to trade with real money...

All traders with forex agree that the switch to real money is a moment of tension. It feels very different to trading on a demo. Psychologically this makes sense. While you're playing around and learning on the demo with fake money – it's a game. But once you put down your notes on the table and make real decisions with those notes, the sweat starts to pour down your back.

It's serious stuff. Your stress levels rise. If you've done the work on your personality you might need to review your weak areas before you progress to this stage. Are you prone to anxiety? Are you likely to takes risks you can't afford? Are you too laid-back to respond to signals when you need to?

There's an urban myth among traders that demo platforms are fixed – so that you're more likely to win. This means that the brokers give you a false idea of how easy it is to trade – and so you're more likely to jump into with a handful of your real live cash.

The fact is that if you've done your research on the forums – you'll have picked a reputable broker. That broker will be a member of a financial regulation institution – like the Financial Services Authority, (FSA) in the United Kingdom, or the national futures authority (NFA) in the US.

Never take on a broker who works without proper regulation. It makes sense. In such a risky market, you have to be sure about the person who is trading your money.

A well-regulated broker is highly unlikely to risk their own reputation by giving you false feedback on your trading decisions during demo time.

Therefore, it's your *perception* of the markets that changes when you start using real cash.

You know you have to make good trades. But if you're wise, you'll be aware that there will be losses. Your strategy should work towards the overall goal of you making a profit. You'll know by now how to minimise your losses with sensible money-management.

Here's a frightening figure. An estimation of the average loss of a newbie forex trader is about $15,000. This is what happens without planning, playfulness and preparation.

How to prepare yourself for trading with money

As already mentioned, you should make sure you know your characteristic way of dealing with stress. And fix any false assumptions about your own ability.

- Have you studied the details of forex until you're sure you understand it?
- Have you actually traded with profit for three months in a row?
- Do you know which signals work for you?
- Have you been realistic about the amount of money you can afford to invest?
- Have you researched your chosen broker in depth?
- Are you taking an intelligent approach towards the amount of leverage you've taken on?

Be thorough. Check everything. Get some sleep.

Step Four: Practical assessment: How are you doing – *honestly?*

I can't emphasise this enough – you've got to look at your own progress with total honesty. This is as important as all your previous learning, working with your strengths and practising on demos.

From a psychological point of view, it's natural to think you're better at something than you are. We all like to think well of ourselves. We often over-estimate our own ability and skill.

Don't fall into this trap. If you do you're more likely to take stupid risks – especially if you're trying to follow a bad trade with a good one to make the money back. Keep detailed records of your trades.

Watch out for the temptation to trade late at night. It's easy to do this if you're trading in a currency that has a different time zone.

The effects of tiredness on the functioning of the brain is much worse than it might appear. Generally speaking your reflexes, pattern recognition, perception and attentional ability will be much lower. You won't be able to concentrate to the level you need when the signal comes in. Add to that the fact that you might get into rough seas and be desperate to put it right – and before you know it – you're in an extremely vulnerable position.

Have a look at your performance as if you were assessing a stranger. If you've lost your allotted amount of cash – stop trading.

Go back to the demo platform. Relax and play around again. Find out what went wrong with your approach. You might have been relying on the wrong signals. If so, consider using an automated system – but find one with a good reputation among other traders. Or just find another source.

Ask questions. Post on forums or better yet, discuss your methods with a forex partner – even a group of local fellow traders. If you're lucky enough to be part of a group nearby, spend some time with a trader who is making good trades. Watch and learn. Talk about their approach and see if you can make it work for you.

Now you know the basics of how to start in forex.

All these goals, steps and outlines will give you a significant edge – because so many of those who fail at forex don't do any of them. But what could give you the ultimate edge in this market?

Thinking like a successful trader.

The deep psychology of success applies in all areas of business. And here, I've applied it specifically to forex. That's what we'll look at in the next chapter.

Chapter Four:

The Deep Psychology of Trading Part 1:

how to *think* like a successful trader

Your ultimate weapon in the battle to win at forex trading is in your own mind. Some people are born with a feel for business success. It doesn't matter what kind of business they get into – somehow they make it work.

There's no mystery to this. Psychologists have researched this area and realised what kind of thinking these successful men and women do. And it doesn't matter if you don't have it already. Because it can be learned!

The myth of the fearless risk-taker

One of the myths going around is that forex traders who work it properly – are cold, calculating risk-takers.

This is entirely wrong, because to think like a real trader is to think clearly – combining intuition as well as intellect.

Successful traders have a fine-tuned perception of opportunity

Here's the secret to intuitive trading.

A successful trader has a finely-tuned *sense of opportunity.*

They 'see' the right pattern at the right time – and they act on it. They have a heightened sense of pattern recognition. This is no accident. They intuitively spend time just watching, tuning into the markets – observing them as if they're watching birds in flight. That's right. Just watching and learning without thinking too hard.

They've learned enough to understand what they're looking at. But they allow their intuitive mind to observe the market. This is only possible if you do this without goals. In other words – **spend time observing without trading**.

You can train yourself to this level of intuition/intellect mix.

Start this deep psychology training during your time on the demo system. This exercise seems so simple but it'll put you streaks ahead of most other beginners at forex:

- Make sure you know the forex environment of your chosen currency pair inside out.
- Spend some time, an hour or so - just watching the charts in a relaxed and calm way
- Observe the movement, the flow of prices

Copyright Jill Harris © 2011

- Absorb this movement of prices as they flow across your screen – without trading at all
- While you're doing this – focus on the patterns as they change – but don't try and analyse too deeply
- Write down what you saw and felt in your forex notebook afterwards
- Ask yourself questions on the page
- What details jumped out?
- What patterns seemed to emerge?
- What surprised you?
- When did you notice your attention drifting – and why?

Do this exercise often. It's a good one to do when you've traded in your allotted time-frame for that day or that week – and you're in a calm state of mind.

Good traders are self-aware

They are honest about their mistakes during their time on the demo platforms. They don't mind practising the skills they need to improve. They work towards a state of excellence by setting their own pace.

If it takes you six months on the training platforms to get a feel for trading – then do it.

If it takes a year before you can produce three profitable months in a row – then that's how long it's going to be. Thinking like a trader means gaining a **high level of competence** –

and knowing that every moment you spend doing this worthwhile.

This is the kind of patience you need. But it doesn't mean you have to repress the desire to trade – you just have to re-frame the whole idea of patience. Your desire should be directed at reaching a peak performance. You're in training – for as long as it takes.

Think of an athlete. Training, training, training. It takes four years to train for an Olympic games. There's no other way if you want to make the grade. Of course an athlete has to have a fair level of fitness and ability before she can even qualify for the training.

If you're going to change your thinking so that it's the same as a successful trader – you need to absolutely clear about one thing. YOU HAVE TO STICK TO THE PLAN.

A successful trader becomes skilled in every area related to forex

Whether it's learning the basics, observing the markets or trading on a demo, you should be constantly aware of your own level of competence. If you get stuck on something – don't move on until you feel you've mastered it. Make sure your focus is very specific – right from the start. For example, plan to:

- Pick a single currency pair and stick with it.
- Pick a trading time-frame and stick with that too.
- Pick your exit levels and set them in stone!

Copyright Jill Harris © 2011

Once you feel you've really got a handle on one of the areas in your preparation development plan – move on. Set yourself a time-frame for trading – as soon as you start the demo. Stay with the same currency pair and don't be tempted to chop and change.

Be SPECIFIC. The more specific you are – the more competent and effective your trading will be – because you're narrowing down your learning to a single set of skills rather than over-reaching and missing important details.

When you move on to using real money don't suddenly swap currencies or time-frames. Just because you've found it easy to make profit with fake money – and you fancy branching out – doesn't mean it's a good time to do that!

The deep psychology of success means being able to balance fear with feasibility...

This is the ultimate secret of success. If you can achieve this – and make sure it becomes second nature to you – you'll be more likely than most to succeed on the forex.

Fear is the root of anxiety and impatience.

You must recognise the fear – and prepare for it. Forex is a risky market. But your fear should keep you alert – not overwhelmed.

The deep psychology of working with your fear is to know your personality type. And make sure you know when fear is taking over - because that's the time to stop trading.

Copyright Jill Harris © 2011

Feasibility – is the art of knowing something can be done. If you've studied the theory, stuck to specifics and played on the demo until you make profits more than losses – you know it's doable.

An assessment of your own feasibility is only possible if you've honest with yourself about your progress.

Remember – to think like a successful trader you need a balance of feasibility with fear.

Feasibility <---------------------------------------> **Fear**

And you also need to be tuned into profitable opportunities. Practise these skills as much as you can every time you're doing anything connected to forex.

The successful trader is aware of her desire – her hopes of success. At all times

I'm not just talking about wishful thinking.

You can dream of making a million, but it's perhaps more helpful to feed your mind with thoughts of competent, successful trades based on your own skills. That way it won't be such a difficult challenge to master the skills you need.

If you keep sight of your hopes and goals, then everything becomes part of your overall plan.

From your first sight of candlesticks (don't ask – you'll have to discover that one for yourself!) to the hour you spend just observing the markets looking at the patterns – you'll be constantly aware of your hopes.

You hope to become good at forex.

You hope to know everything you need to know in order to master the art of trading.

You hope to spend time understanding the technical aspects of analysis so that it doesn't phase you.

Because of your goals – you understand it isn't just about making money – it's just as much about the journey towards skilful trading

You desire all these things every step of the way...

Oh, and in the end of course – you do hope to make a profit – that's for sure!

A successful trader at forex is goal-orientated

To think like a good trader, you have to have a plan and stick to it. I know I've said this before but it really does separate the wheat from the chaff.

Keep notes. Re-visit your plans, your goals - and work on your outline of a great strategy - one that suits your temperament.

The more you learn about forex, the more you'll begin to understand the different kinds of strategies traders are using. Find one that fits your character type. Plan your money-management goals and do not waver from them.

Thinking like a successful trader means being creative too!!

Work within your strategy – there's always scope for tweaking as you learn more. Your experience of failed trades are useful for teaching you how to make small, thoughtful changes to your position in the market.

If you approach forex as a business – you'll find it helps if you're flexible within your own financial boundaries. This works particularly well if you've got a forex buddy with similar goals. Choose your trading friend carefully – and make sure she reads this book too. Then you'll both know where you're coming from as far as attitude, goals and competence are concerned.

You'll also know each others' character type. And you'll give invaluable support to each other when characteristic weaknesses begin to surface!

Chapter Five: The Deep Psychology of Trading Part 2:

how to trade in the long term – successfully

The deep psychology of long-term success in forex is to continue thinking in successful way.

Remember, there's no difference in the level of risk-taking behaviour between a successful trader and the general public. If anything, they are more risk averse.

They base their behaviour on the **feasibility** <----------------------------> **fear** balance.

They also are flexible enough to:

- Know how to deal with losses
- Constantly update their knowledge about the markets
- Keep to a working strategy long-term
- Creatively plan for any future changes they wish to make
- Keep their desire for profit realistic
- Understand who they are
- Understand what happens in group psychology

How to deal with lossess

Know right from the start that you will make mistakes. A good trader accepts her mistakes – and does not arrogantly suppose that she is immune to them just because she's made a few profitable trades in the past and has studied the forex market hard.

One of the best ways to learn acceptance is through regular meditation sessions. Keep to the simple breathing meditation we discussed earlier.

Mistakes are what make you good – in the long-term. You learn. Make sure you've always got an eye on your risk-management plan. If your stop-losses are sensible – you'll never lose more than you can afford.

This is how to minimise your losses:

- Plan your money-management system in advance
- Don't change your mind about your stop-losses half-way through a trading session!
- In other words – always stick to your exit point
- Create 'limit orders' on your exit point – this means that you're not able to do it manually
- If you believe you've learned enough to widen your gap – practice it first on a demo
- Better still – don't widen your gap at all – keep it simple

Constantly update your knowledge about the markets:

It's the same with any subject. The more you study it – the more you realise you don't know. Keep asking questions – and find the answers on forums and from knowledgeable forex friends.

Learn who the really good traders are. Consider perhaps paying for a course they run once you're serious about this business.

Stay alert to any changes in the fundamentals. What is happening in the economies of your chosen currencies? It doesn't matter how good you are on the technical analysis – you must never forget you're in a volatile, sensitive market.

Keep an open, enquiring mind about everything to do with forex.

Avoid scams like the plague. A great website for giving you information about current scams, especially automatic signals systems scams is www.forexdarkside.com .

Visit it often, and check out any news about rogue brokers on www.forexpeacearmy.com.

Don't forget to carry on observing the market – without trading. Accustom your brain to patterns. See how they form over the long term. If you think you're seeing something interesting and repetitive – you're right!! It's called an Elliott wave. More on that later.

Copyright Jill Harris © 2011

Keep to a working strategy long-term

If it works, don't get bored with it. Of course, the more experience you have, the more possibilities you'll see. And this is how it should be – that's one of the deep psychological methods of success.

The thing is – it takes time and practise to know when to change your strategy. You might think your forex radar is good – but you could be heading for disaster. Remember to keep things realistic.

Don't expect to make millions.

Plan to make a profit.

And if you *are* making a profit, stick with what you're doing for a serious amount of time before you change your strategy.

Creatively plan for any future changes you wish to make

Investigate any new information that comes your way – new ways of reading the charts or using signals. Be a forex detective. Explore all the possibilities you can think of - in your head and on paper.

Write any new ideas down in your forex notebook – which should never be far away during trading sessions.

Formulate new ideas on paper.

Practise them on demos.

Just don't chop and change because you think you could make a lot of money fast. That's the path of no return. It's not the psychology of success.

Once again, use the forums on reliable sites. See if anyone is using the same concepts you've dreamed up. It could be that you've slipped into a feverish dream and someone will put you right. Or you might be onto something.

Check everything out. Don't lose control. That's the losers' psychology.

Keep your desire for profit realistic...

You probably won't get filthy rich trading forex. Don't fall for that dream. Be realistic – and know what is feasible. It's realistic that if you learn the basics, spend time trading on demos, choose a broker with care, plan and keep to your money-management strategy wisely - you'll make a profit overall.

It's all too easy to get carried away.

If you trade when you're tired and you haven't fixed limit orders on your exit point – well, you'll only have yourself to blame if you crash and burn.

Understand who you are...

Individual psychology is the study of the individual in terms of character, intellect, attitudes and cognition. Know yourself. Explore your personality type.

Who are you? Make sure you're very clear about the answer to this. It's the root and branch of your success.

Don't forget to work with your personality type – not against it. Don't try and be an enthusiast if you're primarily an investigator. Make sure you've got a handle on your weak points – before you step into the market with real money.

Some of the advice out there when it comes to individual psychology is just plain wrong. There are many traders who will tell you that an experienced and successful trader – trades without emotion...

This is psychologically impossible.

Even sociopaths have some emotions.

If you try to act as though you don't feel anything – you'll fail because you'll take too many risks or lose out on your intuitive/creative strengths.

In forex, as in science, there is no such thing as objective observation.

What people are trying to say when they talk about trading without emotions is this:

An experienced trader with a good balance of feasibility <----------------->fear, a fine-tuned radar for the markets, an in-depth knowledge of forex, a tried and tested strategy that they're comfortable with – and who is working with her strengths – won't fall victim to extreme highs and lows whilst trading.

She might think she's acting without emotion.

She's not. She's feeling **calm**.

Feeling calm is an emotion!!!!

And it's one you can achieve – whatever your personality type. If you're naturally a bit hyper, meditation is an essential part of your program for success. If you'll more laid-back, just stick to the plan – and expect calmness to arrive with experience. A calm trader has her radar tuned, her fear nicely balanced with all that learning and expertise.

Copyright Jill Harris © 2011

Anyone can become a calm trader.

- Calmness comes with confidence.
- Confidence comes from experience.
- Experience comes from a long learning curve.
- Learning comes from using your deepest cognitive processes.

Cause and effect! Hey presto, there we are. That's all the deep individual psychology you need to know.

Repressing your emotions and pretending you don't have any is impossible. Forced objectivity is an emotional time-bomb – so don't believe anyone who says they don't feel a thing when they trade. Either they're lying or they don't realise that being calm is just another emotion – and it's an indicator of their level of experience and confidence.

Or they're a robotic sociopath and you should avoid taking their advice at all costs!

Understanding what happens in group psychology... the Elliott wave

Often, when I read about the psychology of trading – written by non-psychologists – they talk about how the market is driven by psychology. But this is too vague to be of any value. Psychology as we've seen – is a huge subject. The complexity of human mind and behaviour is not just one thing.

Copyright Jill Harris © 2011

When looking into the psychology of mass market movements - what you see is a certain type of group behaviour.

Individuals often behave differently in crowds. I won't go into details, but it's important to understand that if you're aware of this tendency – you can break out of it. A large group has a sort of hypnotic effect on most people.

This is where the Elliott wave comes in. I

t's exciting and interesting – and I really recommend that you have a good look at it. Okay, so it's only a theory, but it seems to work. And from a trading point of view – it's a great way to plan your trading decisions once you've reached a certain level of competence.

I'll explain it very briefly here:

- The market acts in a wave-like motion
- It rises and falls in a predictable fashion – based on the group urge to buy and sell at certain points
- The rise takes place in 5 wave forms – and often wave 3 is the most extended
- It falls in three wave forms – a, b and c
- It's a pattern, a bit like fractals in nature (go on, research fractals – they're amazing!)
- It takes a lot of observation to spot these patterns
- If you recognise the pattern, spot the possibility ahead and act in a contrary way to

the group – you'll often make good, profitable trades.

- In other words – learning to ride the Elliott wave is not only profitable it's also deep psychology, man!

I hope I've made you curious about this amazing group phenomenon. Exploring and learning about Elliott waves will give you a real insight into the group psychology of any market. It works especially well with forex.

Once you've got an idea of what an Elliott wave looks like – go and do some observation on a demo platform – remembering not to trade while you're looking at patterns. See if you spot the real thing.

It's fascinating to watch the wave unfurl. If you've a creative personality type, a helper/socially aware type or an investigator type – you'll probably find it easier to spot them than others.

But don't worry if you can't see the wave for the sub-waves. Find another strategy – one that works well with you. But remember that the waves are there. And that's deep group psychology.

Conclusion

In this book you've learned about the deep psychology of success.

You've discovered what steps you need to take in order to become proficient at forex trading.

You've found out that successful traders share a group of behaviours that can be learned – such as:

- Recognising opportunities

- Feasibility/Fear balance

- Normal attitudes to risk

- A fine-tuned radar for their particular market

- A desire to become competent in forex

- A wish for success – they're goal driven at all stages of the process

- Self-awareness

- Calmness – based on experience

- A realistic approach to money-management

- A realistic approach to achievable levels of profit

- An understanding of group psychology in market situations
- An attitude of continued learning

Now you know all this – you might decide that forex is not for you.

It takes work – and time. It's a big learning curve. You'll need to take on the challenge of learning a lot of information. You won't be able to trade with real money for a long time. You'll need to practise like an athlete. You'll need to focus on economic changes, social upheaval and all kinds of international politics to get a handle on your chosen currencies.

You'll also have to get a handle on yourself.

You might decide you don't want to look too deeply at who you are. You might not want to know what your weaknesses are – not everyone can accept they have any at all!

On the other hand, you might decide to take everything you've learned about yourself – and the deep psychology of success – and apply it to a different kind of business. Something that suits you better.

Great. It's far wiser to realise right from the start that forex doesn't suit your personality.

Who knows, if you do your research and find some business that works with your character – you'll be even more successful than you ever dreamed. It's never a waste of time to expore your self and work on developing a healthy ego.

You can use the deep psychology of success in any area of your life. And I wish you well – whether you stick with forex or not.

Or you might just decide that psychology is a load of mumbo-jumbo and you'll go buy that automatic system – the one telling you it's possible to start earning a million dollars right away...

But I hope you don't do that.

Instead, I hope that everyone who reads this book and decides to take on forex as a serious business model – is a success. And if they truly understand that success rests wholly on a true understanding of deep psychology – I won't need to wish them luck.

They'll make their own luck. Through hard work, an open mind, sensible money-management and an ability to enjoy the ride!!!

Oh, and never forget. Forex is a high-risk place to put your money. Know your stuff. Know yourself. And take care.

www.ingramcontent.com/pod-product-compliance
Lightning Source LLC
Chambersburg PA
CBHW071305170526
45165CB00003B/1435